D1297096

DISCARDED
From Nashville Public Library

YO-YOs

Tricks to Amaze Your Friends

by Ingrid Roper
illustrated by Alan Tiegreen

HarperCollinsPublishers

For Chris

The author gratefully acknowledges the assistance of Stuart Crump Jr. (aka Professor Yo-Yo), editor, *Yo-Yo Times* newsletter; founding editor, *Yo-Yo World* magazine; and author of *It's Yo-Yo Time!*, a book of more than 350 new yo-yo tricks, tips, articles, and stories.

Yo-Yos: Tricks to Amaze Your Friends

Text copyright © 2001 by Ingrid Roper

Illustrations copyright © 2001 by Alan Tiegreen

All rights reserved. No part of this book may be used or reproduced in any manner whatsoever without written permission except in the case of brief quotations embodied in critical articles and reviews. Printed in the United States of America. For information address HarperCollins Children's Books, a division of HarperCollins Publishers, 1350 Avenue of the Americas, New York, NY 10019.

www.harperchildrens.com

Library of Congress Cataloging-in-Publication Data

Roper, Ingrid, date.
    Yo-Yos: tricks to amaze your friends / by Ingrid Roper ; illustrated by Alan Tiegreen.
        p.   cm.
    ISBN 0-688-14663-5 — ISBN 0-688-14665-1 (pbk.)
    1. Yo-Yos—Juvenile literature. [1. Yo-yos.] I. Tiegreen, Alan, ill. II. Title.
GV1216.R65   2001   00-040888
796.2—dc21   CIP
                                                                                          AC

1 2 3 4 5 6 7 8 9 10
❖
First Edition

CONTENTS

THE HISTORY OF YO-YOS

The yo-yo is the second-oldest known toy,
after the doll.

Unlike the more recently invented home video game (1972)
or teddy bear (1906), the yo-yo has been around for thousands
of years. Historians believe an up-and-down toy, the mother
of our modern yo-yo, was invented in China more than 2,500
years ago. The Chinese toy looked very different from the one
you play with now. Chinese children spun two wooden disks
held together by a grooved axle, and they yanked on a plant
vine instead of a string.

Somehow the Chinese
toy traveled to ancient
Greece. The Greeks
called their spinning
toys *disks* and crafted
them from wood, metal,
stone, bone, and
painted terra-cotta.

The Chinese
and the Greeks
played with
the toy, but when
it came to the
Philippines,
possibly in the
1500s, legend has
it that the yo-yo

served as a weapon. According to popular myth, Filipino hunters would wait in trees for an unsuspecting animal and hurl a rock tied to a long heavy rope or vine down at their prey. If the hunter missed, he could pull the rock back up and try again.

The Filipinos also gave the famous toy its modern name. In Tagalog, the Filipino language, yo-yo means "come, come," although it is sometimes translated "come back." This name would not arrive in America until the 1920s.

In European courts the toy entertained princes and kings. In the 1700s French adults and children whiled away hours spinning the toy they called a *jou-jou*, *quiz*, and *incroyable*, which literally means "incredible." A portrait hangs in a French museum of four-year-old Prince Louis XVII dangling his quiz. In England the British royalty loved the toy, which they called a *bandalore*. As a young boy, the future king George IV was such a yo-yo expert that the British also called their yo-yo the Prince of Wales toy.

European travelers eventually brought the yo-yo to America. Two inventors from Ohio applied for the first patent for a "better bandalore" in 1866. Other American inventors experimented with various materials for their toys, making bandalores of hard rubber and glass. One even made an edible bandalore, and another created a bandalore with bells. But yo-yos did not become a true craze in America until the late 1920s, when a Filipino immigrant named Pedro Flores played with the yo-yo around the hotel where he worked in California. Flores's tricks quickly caught the attention of friends and hotel guests from all over the country. Soon he received dozens of requests for his hand-carved yo-yos.

Recognizing a potential fad, he launched the Flores Yo-yo Corporation.

The success of the yo-yo was guaranteed when someone showed it to the inventor and businessman Donald F. Duncan, the same man who dreamed up ice cream on a stick and the parking meter. Duncan realized the possibility of this toy and bought Flores's company for $25,000 in 1932. He opened a factory in Chicago and started mass-producing and promoting his wooden yo-yos.

Duncan understood the importance of demonstration to sell the toy. He thought people needed to be inspired by a yo-yo master before they would play with the yo-yo themselves. So he hired Flores and his friends to travel and show off their yo-yo know-how. He also gave tricks catchy names, such as Walk the Dog, and started yo-yo contests, with prizes for state and city champions.

The famous newspaper owner William Randolph Hearst decided Duncan's yo-yos could help sell papers. These two business masterminds joined forces and required yoers to sell newspaper subscriptions before entering some contests, and at one time the *Chicago Herald Examiner* had a yo-yo editor! Celebrities in the 1930s and 1940s posed for pictures playing with yo-yos, and the singer Bing Crosby sang a swinging yo-yo hit.

In 1965 after a long, drawn-out court battle over whether other companies could call their toys yo-yos, a judge ruled that the name had become so synonymous with the toy that any company could use it. Suddenly faced with increased competition and huge legal bills, Duncan went bankrupt. However, Flambeau Plastics bought the Duncan name and still makes and markets yo-yos under this trademark.

Although the yo-yo has had some ups and downs, it keeps coming back—just like the toy itself!

FUN FACTS

- Half a billion yo-yos have been sold since the 1930s.

- The most expensive yo-yo ever was auctioned for $16,000. It was an autographed gift to country music star Roy Acuff from President Richard Nixon.

- Tom Kuhn, a yo-yo entrepreneur and dentist, owns the world's largest yo-yo. It weighs 256 pounds and measures 50 inches by 31½ inches. It is held up by an 80-foot crane, and when it falls it can really yo! It is on exhibit at the National Yo-Yo Museum, located inside the Bird in Hand store in Chico, California.

- The first yo-yo traveled to space on the space shuttle *Discovery* in 1985. Without gravity, the astronauts discovered that when the yo-yo was released, it moved slowly and gracefully along the string but would not sleep.

- In 1992 the second yo-yo in space went along with the shuttle *Atlantis* and circled the globe 127 times, covering 3,321,007 miles. Talk about Around the World!

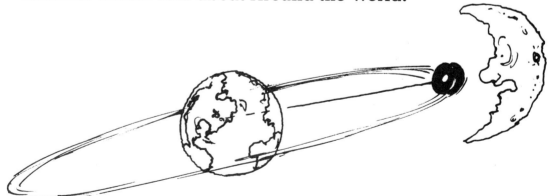

BEFORE YOU BEGIN

KINDS OF YO-YOS
Yo-yos come in a variety of sizes and shapes.
Which one is for you?

TRADITIONAL
This yo-yo is sometimes called classic or tournament and looks like a hamburger bun sliced in half with the string in the middle.

RIM WEIGHTED
This style of yo-yo has weighted outer rims that help create a longer sleeping time. These rims make it easier to perform more complicated string tricks such as Brain Twister.

BUTTERFLY
If you flipped the sides of a traditional yo-yo, you would have a butterfly. This shape makes string tricks such as Man on the Flying Trapeze easier.

TYPES OF AXLES
Choosing the right axle is just as important as your yo-yo shape.

TAKE-APART AXLE
Take-apart yo-yos can be easily taken apart by unscrewing the two halves. This feature makes it easier to remove tangles inside your yo-yo and allows you to change the axle when necessary.

FIXED AXLE
Fixed-axle yo-yos cannot be taken apart without damaging the yo-yo. Although many advanced players prefer fixed-axle yo-yos, experts generally recommend that beginners use a yo-yo that can be taken apart.

CLUTCH YO-YOS
Clutch yo-yos have a centrifugally activated spring clutch. When the yo-yo is thrown down, the force spreads, or opens, the clutch and allows the yo-yo to spin or sleep. As the yo-yo slows down, the clutch gradually closes, grabs the string or the axle, and automatically returns the yo-yo to the player's hand.

TRANSAXLE
Transaxle yo-yos are the latest innovation in yo-yo technology. There are two kinds. In the first, the string attaches to a small plastic sleeve and rotates around the axle, so that the yo-yo string never actually touches the axle itself. The plastic sleeve is made of a low-resistance material that allows incredibly long sleep times, even for beginners. The second kind uses a ball-bearing axle, which makes even longer spin times possible. Experienced yoers have demonstrated record spins of more than ten minutes on one throw of the ball-bearing yo-yo! The long spin times of transaxle yo-yos make them great for beginners who want to learn string tricks such as Elevator or Brain Twister. But transaxle yo-yos do not loop very well.

THE SCIENCE OF YO

HOW DOES A YO-YO WORK?

Two basic scientific principles govern your yo-yo and allow you to perform tricks—*rotational energy* and *friction*. Rotational energy drives the yo-yo on the way down and back up, and friction helps grab the yo-yo to change its direction. When you throw you yo-yo down, energy transfers from your arm, hand, and wrist to the yo-yo to send it down. As the yo-yo reaches the end of the string, it retains this rotational energy from your throw, which causes it to sleep or spin. It will spin inside the string loop until the energy runs out or until you tug it back up again. When you tug on the yo-yo to pull it back up, you increase the friction among the axle, the sides of the yo-yo, and the string, which causes the string to grab the axle and shift the direction of rotational energy. This lets the yo-yo begin the climb back up to your hand.

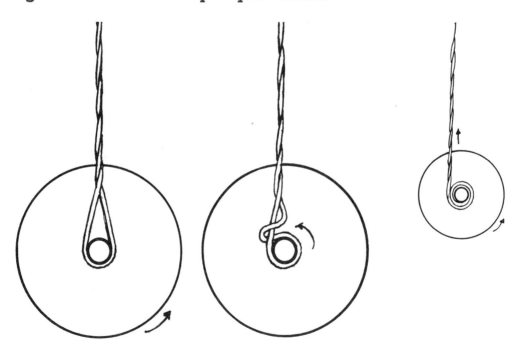

STRINGS

The string is just as important as the yo-yo itself,
because you and the string do all the work!

ADJUSTING THE STRING LENGTH

To find the correct string length, hold the finger loop
end of the yo-yo a little above your waist and let the
yo-yo hang down. Rest the yo-yo on the ground. Put
your finger on your belly button and loop the top of
the string around your finger to determine how much
extra string you will need for a finger loop. Cut the
string so that the yo-yo touches the ground with your
fully extended string at waist height.

TYING THE FINGER LOOP

Fold the top of the string into a small loop over
your finger to determine the size of your finger
loop. Remove your finger and tie a simple
overhand knot to form a small, fixed loop at the
end of the string. Cut off the excess string and throw
it away. Place the slipknot between the knuckles on your
middle finger and pull the knot tightly. The loop should fit
snugly but still be loose enough to remove easily.

POSITIONING THE FINGER LOOP

Slide the finger loop onto your middle
finger between the first and second
knuckles. Putting the string this high on
your finger gives you more power and
makes more advanced tricks easier to
perform.

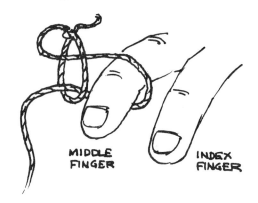

MIDDLE FINGER

INDEX FINGER

WINDING THE YO-YO
Winding up a yo-yo can be frustrating for the beginner. If you're having trouble, try this foolproof solution.

1. Hold the yo-yo in your left hand and place your left finger or thumb over the opening between the halves of the yo-yo.

2. With your other hand, begin to wind the string around the yo-yo. Let it pass over the top of your left finger or thumb one time.

3. Lift up your finger slightly and let the string go directly into the yo-yo for the next two or three winds.

4. Pull your finger out of the loop and finish winding up the yo-yo. Now you're ready to yo!

AVOIDING KNOTS
Even the pros have trouble with knots. Follow these tips to avoid tangles.

1. If you do get a knot, don't swing the yo-yo around, hoping the knot will come out. This will only make any knots worse.

2. Don't use a knife to undo the knot! This is dangerous to your hand, your yo-yo, and the string.

3. Try to pick open the knot with a paper clip or your fingers.

It takes patience to get a knot out. But if your knot really won't budge, it may be time for a new string.

REPLACING THE STRING

The more you use your yo-yo, the more often you'll need to replace the string. If your string is frayed, sticky, dirty, has knots, or has broken, you should definitely replace it! A new string can make tricks easier to perform as well. When you buy your yo-yo, get extra string so you'll be ready. Follow your yo-yo manufacturer's instructions to replace the string.

YO-YO SAFETY

Here are some safety guidelines
every yoer should follow.

1. Practice outdoors when you're learning a new trick—especially tricks such as Forward Pass or Breakaway that put a strain on the string or loop around in large circles.

2. Always check all around you to make sure that your yo-yo won't hit a window, a pet, or a neighbor. Yo-yoing is never a good pastime while you wait for your grandmother to set the Thanksgiving table with her best china.

3. Even as you get more advanced, be careful not to get your yo-yo too close to other people. A swinging yo-yo makes many people nervous.

4. If you are playing to an audience, always warn people to stand back before you try a wide-sweeping trick such as Around the World.

IMPORTANT YO-YO TERMS
Even if you're just beginning, you can talk like a pro.

Yoer
Someone with yo-yo know-how! As soon as you master a few tricks, that will be you.

Dead Yo-Yo
A yo-yo that hangs at the end of the string and doesn't spin.

Flyaway
A yo-yo that breaks its string mid-trick and flies off into the air. Replacing your string whenever it is frayed, worn, or dirty will help prevent this from happening.

Sleeper
When the extended yo-yo spins in its loop at the bottom of the string. This is also known as a Spinner. Most tricks build on this critical skill.

String Tricks
In string tricks the yoer maneuvers the string in, out, and around, as in Man on the Flying Trapeze.

Picture Tricks
Picture tricks are like cat's cradle with a yo-yo. The string and yo-yo are moved around to make pictures, as in Rock the Baby and Eating Spaghetti.

Looping Tricks
These are tricks that send the yo-yo around in circles, as in Loop the Loop and Three-Leaf Clover.

Combination Tricks
Sure, when you're just learning, you perform one trick at a time. But as you advance, you will be able to perform tricks back-to-back in flashy routines. You might show off with Baseball, followed by Breakaway, and then finish it off with Rocket in the Pocket.

Dismount
The way you end your trick and catch the yo-yo back in your hand. For example, a popular way to end Brain Twister is with a Forward Pass.

Non Yo-Yo Hand
Also called your free hand, this is the hand that manipulates the string for some tricks.

BASIC TRICKS

GRAVITY PULL
Start with the most basic of tricks.

1. Hold the yo-yo with your palm facing up and your arm fully outstretched.

2. Toss the yo-yo out over your fingers and straight down toward the floor, keeping your palm facing up.

3. Let the yo-yo fall so that the string goes straight down. The string should flow over the top of the yo-yo, not under the bottom.

4. Before the yo-yo hits the bottom of the string, turn your hand over so that your palm faces down.

5. Jerk the string back up lightly just before the string unwinds all the way. The yo-yo will come back up toward you.

6. Catch the yo-yo in the starting position. Don't worry if you don't get it at first. Keep practicing!

POWER THROW

Pack some punch into your ups and downs.

1. Hold the yo-yo in your hand with your palm up just as you did for Gravity Pull.

2. Bend your elbow and raise your hand so that your yo-yo is at ear level. Your arm will be in power position, as if you're flexing a muscle.

3. Thrust the yo-yo down in front of you with your palm facing up. Stop your hand when it is level with your waist.

4. As the yo-yo falls, flip your hand over so that your palm faces down.

5. Jerk the yo-yo toward you before the string fully unwinds.

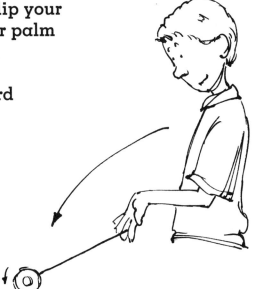

6. Catch the yo-yo with your palm facing down.

FORWARD PASS
The faster you send the yo-yo out, the quicker it comes back.

1. If you are right-handed, stand with your right foot slightly out in front of you. If you're a lefty, put your left foot forward.

2. Begin with your arm down behind your back with your wrist curled up, palm facing back and up.

3. Swing your arm down and forward as you uncurl your wrist.

4. Release the yo-yo when your hand is even with your forward toe. The yo-yo will go out in front of you.

5. Keep your arm straight and fully extended. Once the yo-yo reaches the end of the string, give the string a little tug to bring the yo-yo back to your hand. Catch it with your palm facing up.

It may help to practice this motion without a yo-yo first, to get a sense of flinging your arm out in front of you.

HOP THE FENCE
How many times can you hop the fence?

1. Start with a strong Power Throw.

2. Instead of catching the yo-yo when it comes back up, let it leap over your hand and right back down to the floor.

3. Once you get the yo-yo to hop over your hand once, see how many times in a row your yo-yo can hurdle this fence.

Hopping the Fence will tighten your yo-yo string if you are right-handed and loosen it for lefties. So be sure to tighten or loosen your string accordingly before attempting to do this trick many times.

LOOP THE LOOP
Make your audience swoon with these dizzying loops.

1. Throw the yo-yo the same way you did for Forward Pass, keeping in mind that the yo-yo goes down before it goes out.

2. As the yo-yo comes back to you, don't catch it. Instead, when the yo-yo is about six inches from your hand, move your hand in a small circular motion toward and then away from you with a flick of your wrist.

3. The yo-yo will loop around your hand, come inside your arm very close to your body, and then shoot back out again so that it makes a loop.

4. To catch it, tug the string with your yo-yoing finger and bring the yo-yo back to you. If you stop there, that trick by itself is called Inside Loop.

5. Once you master one loop, try to repeat the loops as often as you can without stopping. Build up to two, three, and then

Throwing an Inside Loop with your right hand will loosen your string one-half twist for every loop. For lefties it will tighten the string. Also, repeated Outside Loops with your right hand will tighten the string but will loosen it with the left. So as with Hop the Fence, tighten or loosen your string accordingly before attempting to do many Outside or Inside Loops in a row.

keep increasing your goal until you can loop the yo-yo twenty-five times or more without a miss.

6. You can Loop the Loop with Outside Loops as well as Inside Loops, and the pros even alternate between the two. To perform an Outside Loop, begin the loop in the same way, but as it comes back to you, flick your hand out and away from you so that the yo-yo circles around the back of your hand.

Loop Off

When yo-yo contests end in a tie, a Loop Off often decides the winner. The contestant who can Loop the Loop the most times takes the prize.

THE SLEEPER

Most tricks build on this one—and the secret is all in the wrist.

1. Begin with a forceful Power Throw. To get the hardest Sleeper possible, throw the yo-yo out in front of you at a forty-five-degree angle. The harder you throw your Sleeper, the longer it will spin at the bottom.

2. Keep your palm facing the floor. Rather than jerking the yo-yo back up toward you when it reaches the ground, relax your wrist and let the yo-yo spin in place at the end of the string. If thrown properly, it should spin, or sleep, for a few seconds.

3. Jerk the string lightly and the yo-yo will come back up to your hand. Getting the yo-yo to sleep is the key to almost every other trick, so keep trying until you get it!

TROUBLE SLEEPING?

If your yo-yo . . .	then . . .
won't come back up	tighten your string
comes back without stopping	loosen your string
doesn't reach your hand on the return	cut down your sleeping time

WALK THE DOG

After you master Sleeper, you're ready to take your hound for a stroll!

1. Throw a hard Sleeper. As the yo-yo goes down, let it slowly and lightly touch the ground.

2. Like a playful puppy pulling on its leash, the yo-yo will roll forward. Walk with it in front of you.

3. Tug the yo-yo back into your hand before it stops spinning. With practice, you can increase how far you walk the dog.

THE CREEPER
This trick builds on Walk the Dog.

1. Throw a hard Sleeper and let it roll out in front of you as if you were walking the dog.

2. Kneel down and lower your hand to the floor.

3. Tug the yo-yo, and it will creep back toward you.

THE DRAGSTER

Give your yo-yo room to travel.

1. Throw a hard Sleeper. Carefully begin to work the string loop off your finger.

2. As your yo-yo sleeps, gradually lower it to the floor.

3. Then let it go! Your yo-yo will zoom out in front of you like a race car speeding for the finish line.

BREAKAWAY
This sweeping shoulder-to-shoulder arc defies gravity.

1. Practice this trick outdoors. Make sure both sides of you are clear.

2. Bend your arm as if making a muscle, as you would for a Power Throw, except turn your elbow out to the side.

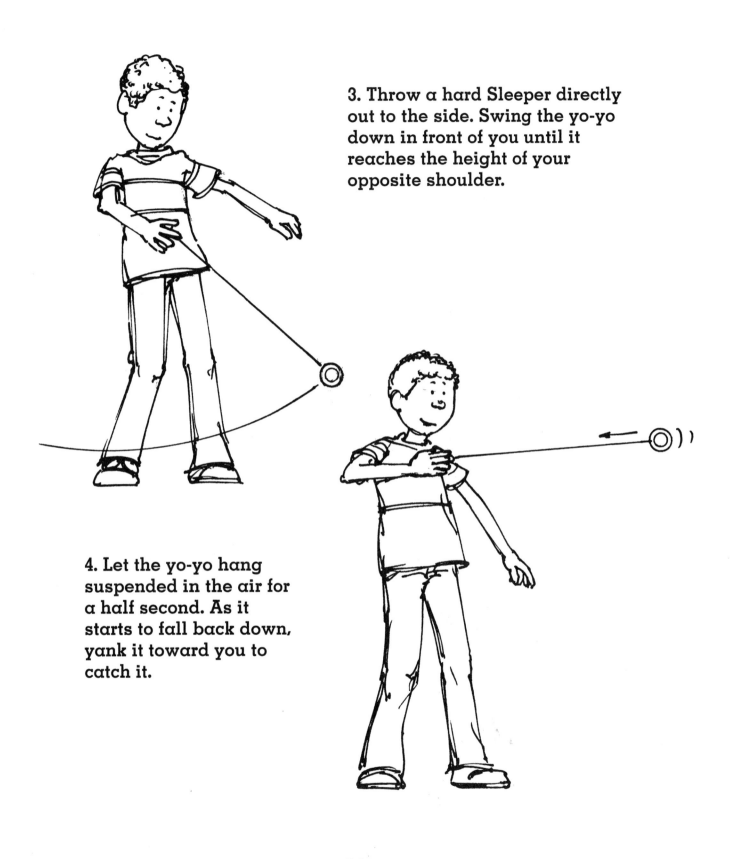

3. Throw a hard Sleeper directly out to the side. Swing the yo-yo down in front of you until it reaches the height of your opposite shoulder.

4. Let the yo-yo hang suspended in the air for a half second. As it starts to fall back down, yank it toward you to catch it.

AROUND THE WORLD
Give yourself at least six feet on every side for this whirlwind journey.

1. Check behind and in front of you in a safe, open area outdoors. Make sure you are far away from windows, glass, your pet turtle, and, of course, friends, family, and innocent bystanders.

2. Throw a Forward Pass straight out in front of you.

3. Instead of pulling the sleeping yo-yo back toward you, swing it up and out in a wide circle.

4. As you bring the yo-yo back around, tug it lightly and it will come back into your hand. While you are learning this trick, make only one circle at a time, or else you might break the string and send a flyaway yo-yo hurtling into the air!

NOT MAKING IT AROUND THE WORLD?

If your yo-yo . . .	then . . .
returns before a full circle	make sure the string is taut as you swing it around
comes back too soon	throw a harder Sleeper

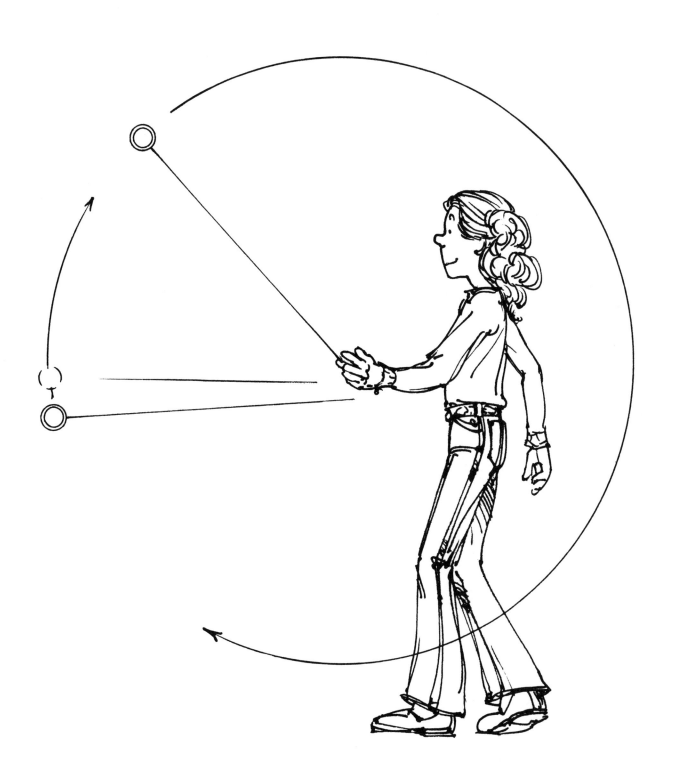

AROUND THE CORNER

Once you've gone Around the World,
stay a little closer to home.

1. Throw a hard Sleeper.

2. Raise your hand as if you were about to testify in court. Make sure your elbow is in front of the string.

3. Quickly drop your hand and forearm so that the string dangles over your upper arm and the yo-yo hangs behind your arm.

4. Reach back with your yo-yo hand and pluck the string between your thumb and forefinger, just above the yo-yo. The yo-yo should jump up and wind over your arm and shoulder.

5. Let the yo-yo unwind fully in front of you, then jerk the string and catch the yo-yo in your hand.

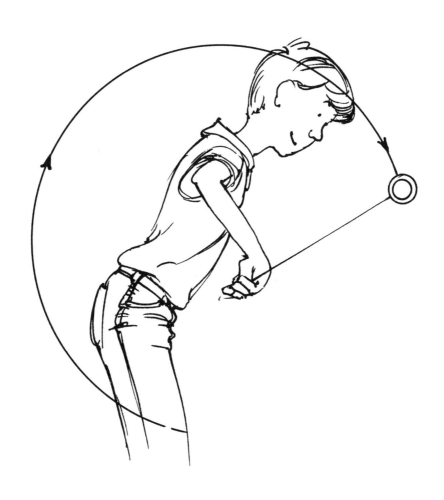

ROCK THE BABY

Master one of the most popular tricks of all time.

1. Throw a hard Sleeper. You will need to make the yo-yo sleep for six to eight seconds.

2. Raise your yo-yo hand up in front of you.

3. With your free hand, lift the string up and out.

4. With your yo-yo hand, pinch the string several inches above the yo-yo.

5. Spread the fingers of your non yo-yo hand through the loop you've created to form a triangle-shaped cradle. Move your sleeping yo-yo back and forth as if it's rocking in the cradle.

6. Let the string go when the yo-yo slows down, and it will wind back up and return for you to catch.

Practice this a few times with a dead yo-yo until you get the feel of touching and moving the string!

INTERMEDIATE TRICKS

DOG BITE
Wear long, baggy pants for this chomper.

1. Spread your legs apart.

2. Throw a fast Sleeper and swing the yo-yo back between your legs.

3. When the yo-yo swings all the way back behind you and the string brushes against your pant leg, raise your leg slightly and give the yo-yo a light tug. The yo-yo will bite your pants. If at first the yo-yo doesn't stick to your leg, try again with a harder, stronger Sleeper.

FLYING SAUCER

You'll soon see why this graceful flight is also called a Sleeping Beauty.

1. Throw the yo-yo out diagonally at an angle across your body. If you throw it correctly, it will seem to sleep sideways. Raise your arm up while the yo-yo rotates on its side.

2. At the same time, gently hook your non yo-yo hand forefinger or thumb around the string and raise it up so that both hands are level. Slowly slide this finger along the string toward the yo-yo until the finger is about three or four inches from the yo-yo. Let the yo-yo rotate on its side. It will look like a flying saucer.

3. Lift the yo-yo up in the air, raising both hands at the same time and releasing the string. The yo-yo will pop back toward you so you can catch it.

BASEBALL
Hit a home run.

1. Throw the yo-yo out diagonally at a forty-five-degree angle across your body so that it sleeps sideways just as it did for Flying Saucer.

2. Bend your knees.

3. Keeping the string taut, let the yo-yo touch the floor and Walk the Dog on its side in front of you in a half circle. For added drama, count out loud as your yo-yo rounds the bases: first, second, third, home run!

4. As the yo-yo comes back to you, catch it, or for a showstopping finish, send it back out again in a Forward Pass before you dismount.

JUMP THE DOG THROUGH THE HOOP
The dog walks under you instead
of in front.

1. Throw a hard Sleeper.

2. As you bring your yo-yo hand down, bring the yo-yo behind your back. Let the dog walk forward between your legs.

3. Rest your yo-yo hand on your hip to form a hoop with your arm. Give the string a little tug so that the yo-yo comes up past your leg, through the hoop, and back into your hand.

ELEVATOR
Going up?

1. Throw a hard Sleeper.

2. Take the index finger of your non yo-yo hand and slowly place your finger on the string.

3. Drop your yo-yo hand down. Gently work the string into the yo-yo opening. Raise your non yo-yo hand up slowly while pulling down on the string with your yo-yo finger. The yo-yo will look as if it's climbing up the string.

4. When the yo-yo is six inches away from your index finger, quickly flip the yo-yo over the top, drop your non yo-yo hand, and catch the yo-yo on the return.

EATING SPAGHETTI

For once you can slurp while you eat!

1. Throw a hard, straight Sleeper.

2. While the yo-yo sleeps at the bottom, take your non yo-yo hand, pinch the string about five inches from your finger, and pull up to form a small loop, like a noodle. Pinch the noodle between the thumb and forefinger of your yo-yo hand. Continue pulling up small loops, until you have only a few inches of string left. This is your heaping pile of spaghetti.

3. Pull the yo-yo up to your mouth. Be sure your hand is between the yo-yo and your mouth so you don't knock out a tooth! Let the pile of string go as you make a loud slurping sound. The string will wind quickly into the yo-yo. It will look as if you swallowed the spaghetti in one big gulp!

DIZZY BABY
Take your baby for a whirl.

1. Throw a hard Sleeper.

2. Perform Rock the Baby. Swing the baby back and forth in the cradle.

3. Flip the yo-yo over the cradle one to three times. On the final spin throw the yo-yo away from you and catch it as it comes back.

Be sure to flip the yo-yo around the side of the cradle that isn't attached to your finger to avoid creating a big knot.

ADVANCED TRICKS

THREE-LEAF CLOVER
Three's a charm.

1. Throw a Forward Pass up and out in front of you to create the first leaf over your head.

2. As the yo-yo comes back, flick your wrist to the inside to throw another Forward Pass straight out in front of you to form the second leaf of the clover.

3. Again when the yo-yo returns, flick your wrist and send the yo-yo directly down toward your toes to form the third leaf. Getting the feel of throwing a Forward Pass toward your feet may take a while to master!

4. Jerk your wrist back to catch the yo-yo in your palm.

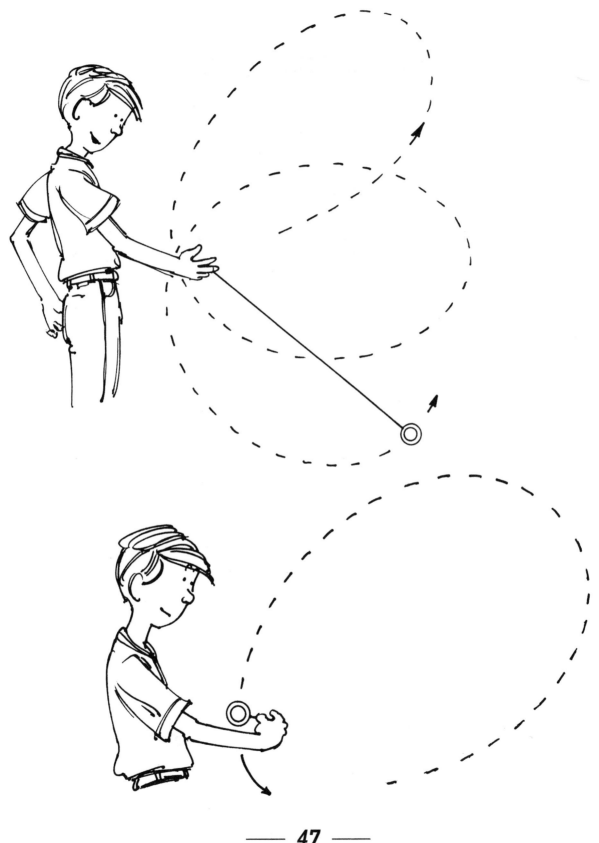

SHOOT THE MOON
Combine a Forward Pass and upward loop for this star.

1. Throw a hard Forward Pass in front of you.

2. When the yo-yo starts to come back, flick your wrist back and up in a circular motion to toss the yo-yo in a loop directly above your head.

3. Tug gently on the string to help the yo-yo wind up as it comes back to earth. When the yo-yo is about halfway down, flick your wrist and send the yo-yo back out in front of you in another Forward Pass.

4. See how many out-and-up loops you can make in a row!

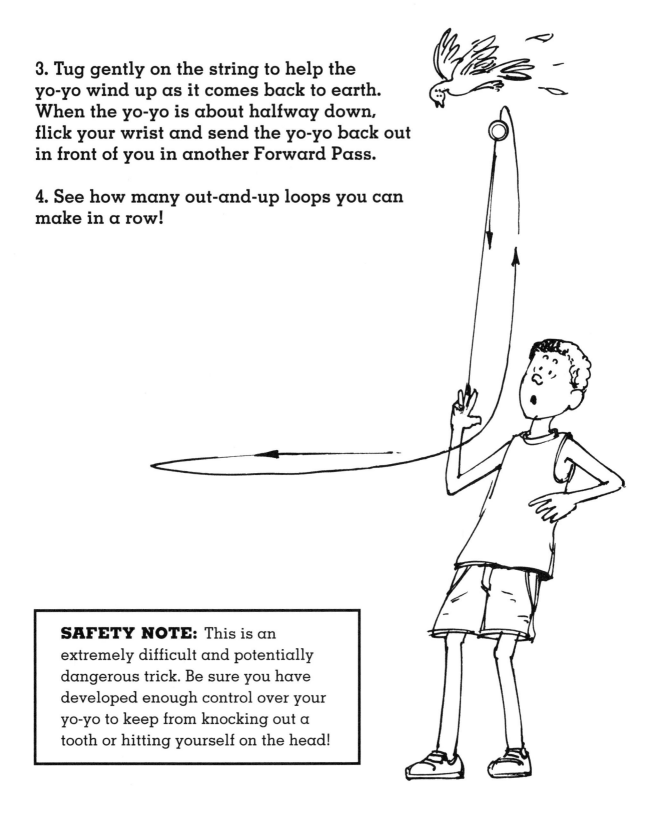

SAFETY NOTE: This is an extremely difficult and potentially dangerous trick. Be sure you have developed enough control over your yo-yo to keep from knocking out a tooth or hitting yourself on the head!

PINWHEEL
Set off some fireworks with this spinner.

1. Start with a Breakaway, throwing the yo-yo out from one shoulder to the other.

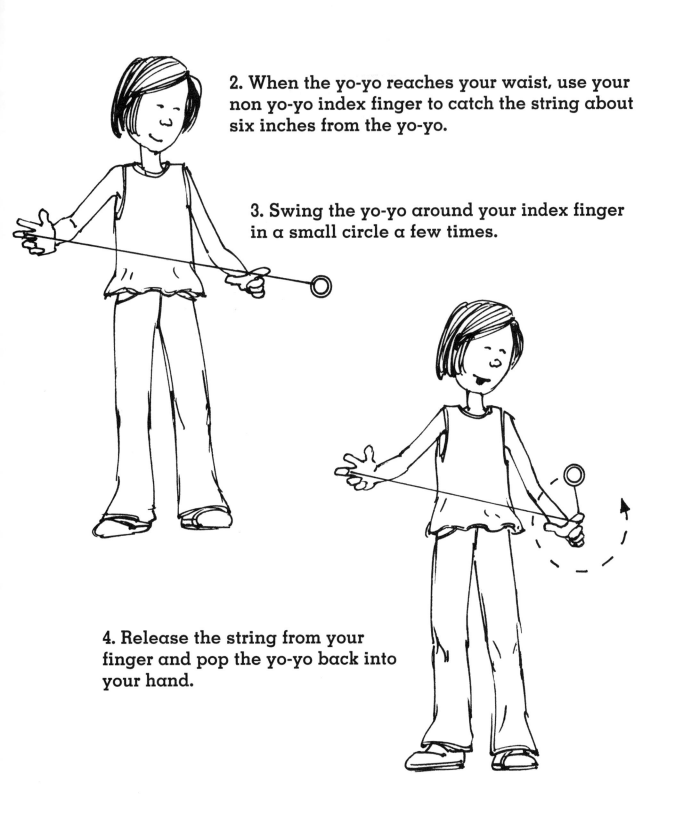

2. When the yo-yo reaches your waist, use your non yo-yo index finger to catch the string about six inches from the yo-yo.

3. Swing the yo-yo around your index finger in a small circle a few times.

4. Release the string from your finger and pop the yo-yo back into your hand.

BRAIN TWISTER

Up, down, and around.

1. Start with a strong, hard Sleeper.

2. Bring the index finger of your free hand in front of you and onto the string.

3. Lift this finger straight up and at the same time pull the string down with your yo-yo hand as if you're doing an Elevator. When the yo-yo is halfway between both hands, insert the string into the yo-yo opening.

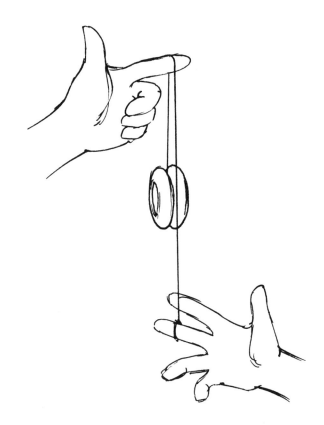

4. Lift the yo-yo up toward you on the doubled string with your yo-yo hand finger. Move your other hand forward and down. The yo-yo will slide up and over and down.

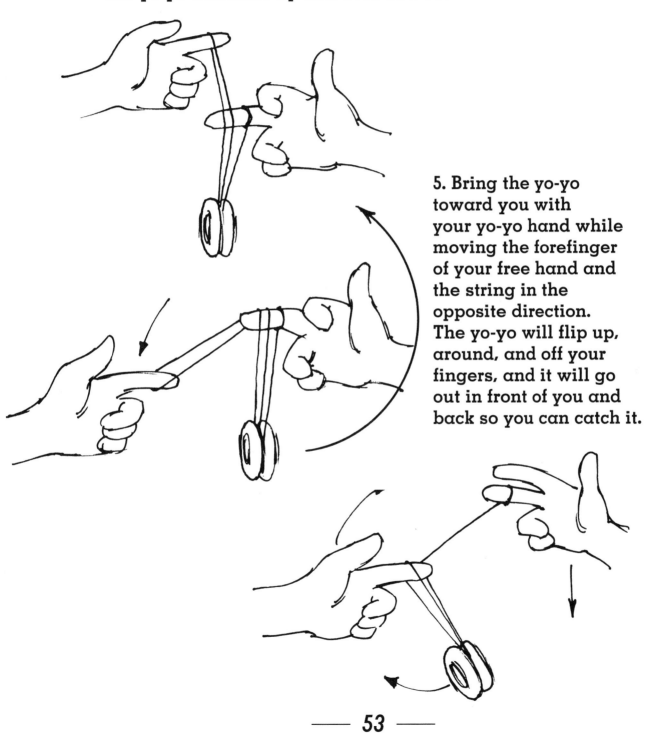

5. Bring the yo-yo toward you with your yo-yo hand while moving the forefinger of your free hand and the string in the opposite direction. The yo-yo will flip up, around, and off your fingers, and it will go out in front of you and back so you can catch it.

MAN ON THE FLYING TRAPEZE
Win applause with this high-wire act.

1. Begin with a Breakaway.

2. When the yo-yo reaches waist height, place the index finger of your non yo-yo hand over the string so that the yo-yo swings up and over your finger.

3. The yo-yo will flip over your finger in an arc. Catch the yo-yo opening on the string.

4. Keep the yo-yo sleeping, and bring the fingers of your two hands together and rock the yo-yo back and forth on the string.

This can be a very difficult trick to master, but don't give up—you'll get it eventually! It's worth the work!

5. Pull your hands apart and then pop the yo-yo off the string and catch it on the return.

SKIN THE CAT
This trick is also called a Tidal Wave.

1. Throw a hard Sleeper. You will need to keep the yo-yo sleeping for six to eight seconds for this trick.

2. Stretch your yo-yo arm out in front of you at waist height, keeping your elbow bent.

3. Reach out and touch the string just below your yo-yo hand with the index finger of your non yo-yo hand. Touch your yo-yo middle finger and the forefinger of your non yo-yo hand together briefly. Pull the string back with your yo-yo hand until your non yo-yo forefinger is about eight inches from the yo-yo.

4. Flip the yo-yo up and out with your non yo-yo forefinger. It will twirl backward around your yo-yo hand.

5. Release your non yo-yo hand and the yo-yo will fly out into a Forward Pass. Catch it on the return.

ROCKET IN THE POCKET

Finish any yo-yo routine with flourish.

1. Practice this trick outside. Check that you are clear on all sides. Be sure to wear a shirt with a breast pocket.

2. Throw a hard Sleeper. Work the string off your finger.

3. Clasp the finger loop between the thumb and forefinger of your yo-yo hand. Give a slight jerk to bring the yo-yo back up the string.

4. When the yo-yo has almost reached your fingers, let go! The yo-yo will soar up into the air and make an arc above your head.

5. Open your shirt pocket to catch the yo-yo on its fall. Bow for the applause from admiring friends and family!

Once you get the hang of it, you can try catching the yo-yo in a pants pocket, your hat, or even in your hand.

DOUBLE OR NOTHING
This masterpiece builds on all your skills.

1. Begin with a Breakaway.

2. Just as in Man on the Flying Trapeze, when the yo-yo reaches your waist, let the yo-yo swing over your index finger. However, keep your two hands level and waist width apart so that the yo-yo flips over the index fingers of both hands.

3. Let the yo-yo continue swinging around so that it winds over your non yo-yo forefinger a second time. When it flips over, catch the yo-yo opening on one of the strings between your hands, as in Man on the Flying Trapeze.

4. To return the yo-yo, flip it gently off the string and remove both fingers from the loops. Let the yo-yo drop toward the floor. Give the string a tug and bring the yo-yo back to your hand.

5. Once you've mastered the Double, you're ready to try Triple or Nothing!

TRICKS WITH TWO YO-YOS

WHIRLYBIRD
Two are better than one.

1. Hold a yo-yo in each hand.

2. Alternate throwing Loop the Loops with each hand. Keep them moving in opposite directions so that as one goes out, the other comes in. Although this is an extremely difficult trick to master, it is well worth the effort because it is the sign of a true yo-yo pro.

CRISSCROSS
Double the fun.

1. Throw Loop the Loop with both hands.

2. Flick your wrists and aim the yo-yos so that they cross in front of you. Alternate your loops so that one yo-yo goes out as the other comes back. Try to keep one higher than the other. When you get the rhythm right, the yo-yos will crisscross in front of you!

3. When you're dizzy, or just ready to stop the mad whirl, tug the yo-yos to return them to your hands.

TANDEM DOG WALK
Give man's best friend a canine companion.

With a yo-yo in each hand, throw hard Sleepers and gently lower the yo-yos to the ground. Walk your two little doggies across the floor.

WHERE TO FIND MORE
Here are some additional yo-yo resources.

ORGANIZATIONS

The American Yo-Yo Association
Founded by yo-yo champion Dale Oliver, the American Yo-Yo Association caters to enthusiasts. You can become a member, find out about clubs and competitions, subscribe to their newsletter, get tips on performing tricks and tuning your yo-yo, and find links to yo-yo destinations across the Internet.
12106 Fruitwood Drive
Riverview, FL 33569
www.ayya.net

National Yo-Yo Museum
This comprehensive museum houses the collection of the Donald F. Duncan family and the Dr. Tom Kuhn Collection, as well as thousands of other items that trace the history of the yo-yo. The museum is located inside the Bird in Hand store, and admission is free.
320 Broadway
Chico, CA 95928
(530) 893-0545
www.nationalyoyo.org

NEWSLETTERS

Yo-Yo Times
P.O. Box 1519
Herndon, VA 20172
www.yoyotimes.com
One-year subscription (4 issues) $12

Send a self-addressed, stamped envelope with first-class postage for a sample copy, or request one by e-mail at YoYoTime@aol.com.

The Noble Disk
124 Cabot Street
Portsmouth, NH 03801
(603) 427-2473
www.cybertours.com/nobledisk
One-year subscription (4 issues) $10

BOOKS

Alton, Bill. *Care and Operation of the Noble Disk*. Portsmouth, NH: Noble Disk, 1998.
A collection of the best from the author's yo-yo newsletter, *The Noble Disk*.

Cassidy, John. *The Klutz Yo-Yo Book*. Palo Alto, CA: Klutz Press, 1998.
Well-illustrated guide for beginners.

Cook, Chris. *Collectible American Yo-Yos, 1920s–1970s: Historical Reference & Value Guide*. Spokane, WA: Collector Books, 1997.
Guide for collectors.

Crump Jr., Stuart. *It's Yo-Yo Time!* Herndon, VA: Creative Communications, 1999.
More than 350 new yo-yo tricks as well as stories and articles about the world of yo.

———. *The Little Book of Yo-Yos*. Philadelphia, PA: Running Press, 1997.
A basic introduction to yo-yoing.

———. *Yo-Yos: 45 Tricks and Tips*. Lincolnwood, IL: Publications International, 1999.
Trick book for beginners.

The Duncan Trick Book. Middlefield, OH: Duncan Toy Co., 1985.
A basic introduction with insight into Duncan yo-yos.

Feser, Neil. *The Book of Yo*. Omaha, NE: Insight Presentations, 1999.
How to achieve the State of Yo.

McBride, Mark. *The Yonomicon*. Tallahassee, FL: Infinite Illusions, 1998.
Breaks down the art and science of yo-yoing into its basic components
and explains the theory and practice of tricks.

Meisenheimer, Lucky. *Lucky's Collectors Guide to 20th Century Yo-Yos*.
Orlando, FL: L.J.S. & S., 1999.
Guide for collectors.

Sayco, Larry. *The Ultimate Yo-Yo Book: 20 Great Tricks and Tips*. New York:
Grosset & Dunlap, 1998.
Beginners' guide to the yo-yo.

Ten Eyck, John E. *The Yo-Yo Book & The Yo-Yo*. New York: Workman, 1998.
A beginners' guide to the yo-yo that includes a fixed-axle wooden yo-yo.

Weber, Bruce. *You Can Yo-Yo! Twenty-Five Tricks to Try*. New York:
Scholastic, 1998.
Beginners' guide.

Whitten, Ted. *The Illustrated Pro-Yo Trick Bible: Volume I: Beginner*.
Tucson, AZ: Self-published by the author, 1998.
A complete guide to the Playmaxx ProYo for beginners.

Yomega Corp. *The Official Yomega Trick Book*. Fall River, MA, 1998.
A basic introduction with insight into Yomega yo-yos.

Zeiger, Helane. *The World on a String*. Berkeley, CA: Self-published by
the author, 1999.
A yo-yo classic.